P9-DIZ-101

MEDITATIONS

SHAKTI GAWAIN

MEDITATIONS

CREATIVE VISUALIZATION AND
MEDITATION EXERCISES
TO ENRICH YOUR LIFE

NEW WORLD LIBRARY

Meditations © 1991 Shakti Gawain

Published by New World Library
58 Paul Drive
San Rafael, California 94903

Cover design: Kathleen Vande Kieft
Text design: Abigail Johnston
Typography: G&S Typesetters, Inc.

All rights reserved. This book may not be reproduced in whole or in part, without written permission from the publisher, except by a reviewer who may quote brief passages in a review; nor may any part of this book be reproduced, stored in a retrieval system, or transmitted in any form or by any means electronic, mechanical, photocopying, recording, or other, without written permission from the publisher.

First printing, March 1991
ISBN 0-931432-68-5
Printed in the U.S.A. on acid-free paper
10 9 8 7 6 5 4 3 2 1

CONTENTS

Meditations

FOREWORD

This book came about in a very special way. Over the years, we have produced several cassettes of Shakti Gawain leading a variety of different meditations. Several people contacted us to ask if we had transcriptions of the tapes—for various reasons, they preferred the written to the spoken word. The first group was of older people who met regularly; each time, one would lead the group, reading a meditation from one of Shakti's books. They had worked through every meditation in her books, and now wanted transcriptions of her tapes so they could continue reading the meditations to each other.

We thought this was touching, and we had transcriptions of her tapes prepared. When we read them, we found they had the same clear simplicity and heartfelt emotion of all of Shakti's books. They worked so well in print, in fact, that we decided to publish them as a collection.

The material in this book is reprinted from four of Shakti's meditation tapes: Contacting Your Inner Guide, The Male and Female Within, Discovering Your Inner Child, and Expressing Your Creativity. The transcripts of the tapes include an introduction given by Shakti on each topic, followed by a meditation.

There are several ways to use this book effectively:

(1) Sit down with a friend, or several friends, and appoint one person as a reader who guides the others through the meditations, like our friends did. Pause a bit where there are ellipses (three or four dots . . .).

(2) Read through the entire meditation, alone, and then do your own version of the meditation.

(3) Read through a bit of the meditation, relax and do it, and then read a bit more, relax and do it, and so on.

(4) Record the meditations on cassette and lead yourself through them.

Regardless of how you choose to work with the meditations, we're sure you'll find a great amount of material that will be uplifting, inspiring, and empowering.

Enjoy!

Marc Allen
Publisher

MEDITATIONS

CONTACTING
YOUR
INNER GUIDE

◇ ◇ ◇

CONTACTING
YOUR
INNER GUIDE

Most of us in this day and age and in our Western society lead very hectic lives. We have many responsibilities: our work, our families, our friendships, our social, community, and political responsibilities. Even our recreational activities often take a lot of our attention and energy. We are very involved in what's outside us. Most of us are greatly in need of balancing this outward focus by taking some time to go within ourselves. We need to get back in contact with our spirit, with our inner creative source.

I believe that each of us has a deep sense of truth within us, the guiding force that can lead us successfully through our lives. But when we spend most of our time looking outside ourselves, involved so intensely with the outside world, we lose contact with that spirit, with that creative source within us.

In addition, most of us have not been educated to believe in that inner intuitive knowingness. We've been taught to follow outside rules, other people's ideas of what's right and wrong for us or what we need to be doing. As a result, we lose touch with the very core of our being.

We need to take some time to cultivate contact with our inner guide. We need to reeducate ourselves to pay attention to that part of us that really knows. It helps if we can begin to take some regular time for this—even if it's just a few minutes each day or even a few minutes once a week. We need this time to learn to relax our bodies and our minds, to move into the deeper awareness that exists within us.

This takes practice, patience, and support. But it's something that's very natural for us, so as we begin to cultivate this habit we will find it easier and easier to go within. After a while we will begin to find that we crave this inner contact. When we spend too much time looking outward there will be a part of us that will start to pull us inside and demand that we get in contact with our deeper self.

MEDITATION: DISCOVERING YOUR INNER SANCTUARY

This visualization meditation will help you begin to establish the practice of moving your attention within, finding a place of relaxation and peace, and contacting your inner wisdom. Before we begin, I'd like to remind you that any time you are doing a visualization meditation, do it in a way that comes easily and naturally for you. Don't worry if you don't see a visual image when you meditate. Some people are visually oriented; others are more audio- or feeling-oriented. So if you get just a feeling about it or even if you are only thinking about it, do whatever comes naturally and easily for you. Accept this, and relax and enjoy it. Also, if I give you certain suggestions, but what comes to you is something different from what I suggest, trust your own experience. Always go with what feels right for you.

◇

To begin the meditation, get into a comfortable position, either sitting or lying down. If you're sitting, it's good to be sitting with your back straight and well supported in a comfortable chair, with your feet flat on the floor and your hands in a relaxed position. If you prefer to lie down lie flat on your back in a very comfortable, relaxed position.

When you are comfortable, close your eyes and become aware of your body; just notice how your body is feeling right now. . . . If you notice any tense places in your body, gently breathe into those places. Imagine them relaxing and all unnecessary tension releasing and dissolving.

First, put your attention on your feet and imagine relaxing them. . . .

Next, put your attention on your ankles and the calves of your legs and gently relax them. . . .

Now put your awareness in your thighs and your hips. Relax the upper part of your legs and your whole pelvic area. . . .

Gently breathe into the lower part of your body and feel it become very relaxed. . . .

Now put your awareness in your abdomen and your stomach, the area of your internal organs, and imagine all your organs relaxing, functioning easily, comfortably, healthfully, and smoothly. . . .

Relax your chest and relax your shoulders, your arms, your hands, and your fingers. . . .

Put your awareness in your neck and throat, and imagine this part of your body relaxing completely. If there's any tension in this area, imagine it flowing down through your arms and out your fingers, out onto the floor and down into the earth. . . .

And now relax your head, your face . . . relax your scalp . . . relax your ears and relax your eyelids. Relax your jaw. . . .

Let your awareness scan through your entire body, from head to toe, from toe to head, and feel your entire body deeply relaxed. . . . Imagine that you can feel life energy flowing smoothly and freely through your entire body. If any area feels tight or tense, gently release it and feel that energy flowing through it. . . .

Take a deep breath, and as you exhale, release any last holding that you're doing in your body. Feel your body totally relax. . . .

Take another deep breath, and as you exhale, relax your mind. Pretend that your mind is just another muscle in your body that you can now relax. You don't have to hold on to any thoughts. You can let everything go for right now and let your mind become very quiet and slow, even a little bit out of focus. . . .

Take another deep breath, and as you exhale, move your awareness into a very deep place inside of you. . . .

Now imagine that you are walking down a path in some very beautiful, natural environment. You may either see the environment visually, or you may feel or sense or pretend that it's there. As you walk down the path you feel the beauty of nature around you . . . and you feel yourself in an increasingly relaxed state of mind. . . .

Imagine that you come to a clearing or some very beautiful spot, and begin to look around or sense or

feel what this place is like. It's a very special, magical place. Notice what's here. Are there trees? Are
there plants? Is there an ocean or a river? Are you
on a mountain or in a field or in a garden? Let your
imagination tell you what this place is. . . . It's very
peaceful and beautiful and it's also very private and
safe. This is your own personal, inner sanctuary
that you are creating for yourself, inside of you. No
one can come here unless invited. This is your own
private place.

Feel how warm or how cool it is. . . . Is it sunny or
shady or a combination of both? How does the air
feel and how does it smell? What kind of sounds are
there in your inner sanctuary? Do you hear birds
or insects or the breeze blowing through the trees,
or the sound of the ocean? Or is it just very quiet?
Are there any flowers or animals near you? Take
whatever comes to you that feels right and feels
good. . . .

Imagine that you are wandering around your inner
sanctuary, getting to know it, getting comfortable in
it and familiar with it. . . . Find a place in your
sanctuary that feels like a comfortable place to sit

or lie down, and make yourself totally at home there. . . . Feel the beauty and the nurturing quality of nature all around you, and allow yourself to open up and receive that beauty and that nurturing. Imagine that you're like a sponge, simply absorbing and receiving the love and the beauty of Mother Nature. . . .

And now move your awareness into a deep, quiet place inside of you . . . keep imagining going deeper and deeper inside yourself until you come to a place of rest and peace within, where all the cares of the world seem far away. Take a moment to simply let yourself be in that peaceful place within, where there's absolutely nothing you have to do or even think about or figure out, a state of quiet beingness. . . .

In this deep, quiet, restful place within yourself you are in contact with your own deepest wisdom, your own natural inner knowingness, the part of you that's very wise and knows everything that you need and is able to give you guidance in your life, moment by moment. Even if you don't feel it or don't quite believe it, just allow yourself to pretend or imagine that it is there. Whether or not you feel it or believe it, it is always there within you. . . .

If you have questions you want to ask your inner guide, go ahead and ask. . . . Quietly be open to receiving, sensing, or feeling what that wisest part of you may have to say in answer to your question. It may come to you in words. It may come to you in an image. Or it may be just a feeling. Take whatever comes, and allow it to enter your aware-ness. . . . It's all right if you feel that nothing is coming; it may come to you at a later time; it doesn't always come the moment you ask. So ac-cept whatever your experience is right now. . . .

If you have more questions you want to ask your inner guide, do so. You can ask for help, for sup-port, for direction, for love, for clarity—go ahead and ask for whatever you desire or need. . . . Whenever you ask, as soon as you ask, the door will open for you to begin to receive whatever your heart truly desires. So simply assume now that whatever you are asking for is beginning to come to you. It may come in a different way than you expect, but it will come. . . .

When you feel ready, become aware once again of your sanctuary and know that this is a beautiful place you can come to any time you desire. It is within you always. All you have to do is relax, close your eyes, take a few deep breaths, and desire to be there. You can go there any time you want. It will be a place where you can relax and get in touch with that deep, inner wisdom. . . .

For now, say goodbye to your sanctuary and begin, once again, to walk up the path. . . . As you walk up the path, become aware of your body in the room. Feel the room around you. . . . When you feel ready, very gently open your eyes and come back feeling relaxed, energized, and deeply connected with yourself.

MEDITATION:
CONTACTING YOUR
WISE BEING

There are many ways we can learn to tap into the wisdom within us. The previous meditation is one of the simplest and easiest ways to go inside and find that wisdom, that knowingness within.

Another way to tap into your inner wisdom is to allow yourself to make contact with an image of a very wise being who is your advisor, your spirit guide, your helper, your counselor, your guardian angel, whatever you want it to be. For some people it's easiest to do it this way. For many, it's wonderful to have the option of using both meditations, on different days.

This is a meditation to get in contact with the wise being that is a part of you. To do this, go back into your inner sanctuary. And once again, remember, whatever you experience is your own way of doing this, whether you visualize, whether you feel, sense, or just think about it. Take what comes to you easily and trust your own experience as long as it feels right to you.

◇

Find a comfortable place to sit or lie down. Be sure your spine is straight. Get in a position so your body can deeply relax. . . .

Take a deep breath. As you exhale, begin to relax your body. Close your eyes. . . . Take another deep breath, and as you exhale, relax your body a little more. . . . Take another deep breath. As you exhale, imagine relaxing your body as completely as you can. . . . If there are any places in your body that still feel tight or tense . . . where you're holding energy you don't need, put your awareness into those places, breathe into them, and, as you exhale, imagine the tension or the excess energy releasing and draining away so that your entire body feels deeply relaxed. . . .

Imagine feeling the life force, life energy, flowing freely and easily through your entire body, nourishing every cell of your body, releasing the old that you no longer need and replacing it with new, vital energy and aliveness. . . .

Now take another deep breath, and as you exhale, relax your mind. . . . Let go of any problems, preoccupations, cares, or responsibilities that you have on your mind right now—just for a little while. You can always bring these things back when it's appropriate. But for the next few minutes, let them all go. . . . Let your mind grow quiet and move slowly. . . . As thoughts come up in your mind, as they inevitably do, just notice them and then release them. Don't stay focused on the thoughts. Release each thought as soon as you notice it. . . .

Imagine that your mind is becoming very peaceful and quiet, like a still lake or pond, so peaceful there's not even a ripple on the surface. . . .

Take another deep breath, and as you exhale, imagine moving your awareness into a very deep place inside of you. . . . Then imagine you are walking down that beautiful path in nature, feeling the peace and beauty of nature around you. . . . As you walk, you gradually feel more and more relaxed and open . . . and you come, once again, into your inner sanctuary, which may be a meadow, a mountaintop, a spot in the woods, a cave, or a beach—anywhere you desire it to be. . . .

You may find yourself in the same place as before, or it could be a different place. Let it be however you want it to be. But know that this is a very peaceful, beautiful, and safe place for you to be. It's a very private place. It's yours. No one else can come here unless invited.

Take a few moments just to be and feel and see, to be aware of your sanctuary and how it feels to be there. . . . Walk around, feel the air, notice the other living beings, the plants or animals or birds. . . .

And then, find a place in your sanctuary to make yourself very comfortable and at home. You can sit down if you wish. . . .

Now look back toward the entrance to your sanctuary, and imagine that you begin to see or sense or feel the presence of a very wise being who is about to enter. This wise being could be a man or a woman, a child or an animal. Or it might be a color or an ethereal presence. . . .

Begin to feel or picture or sense this wise being as it steps through the entrance to your sanctuary and begins to move toward you. . . . See or feel how old or how young, how big or how small . . . how this wise being moves, how he or she is dressed if it's a person. . . . Most importantly, feel the energy of this wise being as it moves toward you. . . .

As it comes closer, greet the wise being in any way that feels appropriate to you. . . . Trust your own feelings. Allow the wise being to greet you and make contact. You can make contact through words or energetically, telepathically, through touch, or in any way that feels intuitively right. Know that this wise being is here to serve you, to help you in whatever way you need. . . .

The wise being may have a message for you, so ask now if it has something to tell you, in words or in any other way something to remind you of or to tell you or to let you know. And then be open to hearing or sensing or feeling what the message is. . . . If there is something you especially need or want, ask for it, whether it be some words of wisdom or some loving support—whatever it may be, go ahead and ask. . . . Let yourself receive the response that this wise being gives to you. . . .

Now continue to be together in whatever way feels good to you. . . . You may wish to be together without words, or you may want to talk. . . . Allow yourself to receive and fully enjoy this experience. And when you feel ready, complete your contact in whatever way you desire for right now. . . .

If you want to keep the wise being with you in the sanctuary, you can do that. If it feels right for the wise being to leave the sanctuary, if you feel complete with your experience for now, then say goodbye and imagine this being moving back up the path and out of the sanctuary. . . . But know that any time you want to, you can come to this sanctuary, you can ask for your wise being to come and be with you here, and you can ask whatever questions you have or ask for whatever support, guidance, love, or contact you need. . . .

Now once again, look around your sanctuary. . . . Remember that this is a place that you can visit any time you want by closing your eyes, taking a few deep breaths, and desiring to be there. . . .

If you want to sleep after doing this meditation, go ahead and let yourself drift into sleep. . . .

If you want to come out of the meditation, say goodbye to your sanctuary for now and begin to move back up the path. Feel yourself more and more alive, energized, and balanced. . . .

Become aware of your body and how it's feeling now, and become aware of the room around you. . . . When you feel ready, very gradually open your eyes and come back into the room. . . .

◇

If you wish to stay longer with this experience, relax even more deeply and stay with it for as long as you desire. . . .

THE
MALE AND FEMALE
WITHIN

◇ ◇ ◇

THE
MALE AND FEMALE
WITHIN

Each of us, whether man or woman, has male and female aspects to ourselves, male and female energies within us. I believe that one of our most important challenges in life is to recognize and develop both the male and female aspects of ourselves and to bring those energies into balance within our own being.

The idea of male and female energies has been with us for a long time. The eastern philosophies have always talked about the yin and yang aspects of the universe. Not only does each of us have yin and yang within; everything in the universe is made up of yin and yang, the two polarized energies: the active and receptive, positive and negative, light and dark, masculine and feminine.

In the West, Carl Jung did pioneering, exciting work with his concept of the anima and animus. He explained that men have a feminine side, the anima, and women have a masculine side, the animus, and that most of us have strongly repressed these aspects of ourselves and we must come to terms with them.

I have found that some people have an initial resistance to using the words female and male for aspects of themselves because in our culture we have so many preconceived ideas about what these words mean. There's a great deal of emotional charge associated with them. If you're uncomfortable with these words, feel free to substitute the words yin and yang, active and receptive, or any others that appeal to you.

I have a particular way of looking at the male and female: I think of the feminine or female aspect of ourselves, whether we're men or women, as the intuitive part of us. It's the deepest and wisest guiding force within us, the receptive door within us that allows the higher power of the universe to enter. It is through the female that we receive the creative power of the universe. Think of it as the receiving end of the channel, in a sense.

The male aspect is action. It's our ability to take action in physical form in the physical world. It's our ability to do things, to speak, to move our bodies. Think of it as the out-flowing end of the channel. The energy comes in through the receptive feminine door and moves out through the masculine ability to take action.

Those two inner forces working together, the female and the male, form the creative process. When we receive the energy and we express the energy into the world through our inner male, we create something. For example, an artist may awaken with an inspired idea for a painting, an image that is communicated from his inner female, and immediately pick up his brush and begin painting, an action taken by his inner male. Or a mother may feel sudden concern for her child, a warning coming from her inner female, and run into the other room and pull the child away from a hot stove, an action taken by her inner male. Another example is a business person who may have an impulse to contact a certain associate, which would be guidance from the inner female. As a result, he or she would make a call and launch a new deal, action taken by the inner male.

An example of how this works in my life is that when I feel moved to write, the initial impulse comes from the higher power of the universe and reaches me through my female, my intuitive feeling in the form of a prompting: "Gee, I'd like to write something. I have something I want to say." Then it's carried out by my masculine self; I get a piece of paper and sit down and write something. And something is created through the union of the male and female within me, through the female initiating the creativity and the male carrying it forth.

Here's a simple way of putting it: The female in us says, "I feel this." The male in us says, "I hear you—what would you like me to do?" She says, "I want that." He says, "You want that? Okay, great. I'll get it for you." This union of feminine and masculine energies within the individual is the basis of all creation. Female intuition plus male action equals creativity.

For us to live a harmonious and creative life, we need to have both energies functioning fully and completely, and working together. It's necessary for us to put the female energy in the guiding position. Her natural function is as our guide. The female energy is tuned in to the higher intelligence of the universe. Naturally we want to be guided by that highest intelligence. The function of the male energy is to listen to that intelligent guidance and to figure out how to carry it out in the world. The true function of male energy is clarity, directness, and a passionate strength based on what the universe inside of us, coming through our female, tells us.

It's important to remember that I'm talking about an internal process. People sometimes become confused and upset because they externalize what I'm saying. They think I'm saying that women should tell men what to do, that men should listen to women for their guidance, that men should do everything for women. That's not what I'm saying—I'm saying that within each of us, the feminine aspect of our being, which is the inner guidance, needs to be the initiating energy, and the masculine aspect is the energy that carries out our inner knowingness.

The idea of male and female is really just another way of saying that we need to listen to our own truth, our own knowingness, and be willing to act on it.

When we take the concepts of male and female energies and project them externally, we become confused. A lot of the stereotyped ideas of feminine and masculine energies really apply to how they're meant to function internally, but we have tried to make them function externally by saying women are supposed to be this way and men are supposed to be that way. And then we limit ourselves: Women play out only the feminine energy and men play out only the male energy. We need to have both. Internally, each individual is a complete male/female being.

Sometimes people feel afraid when they hear about this idea. They fear we're all going to end up alike. If we're complete masculine/feminine beings we're all going to be androgenous. I haven't found that to be true. What I find to be true is that when a woman allows her male energy to support her internally, when she starts trusting that male energy, she feels safer to become more feminine, to become more open, softer, more emotional, more receptive, knowing her masculine strength will support and take care of her. Likewise, when men allow themselves to feel the power of their feminine energy, it enhances their masculinity. They feel stronger, they feel more powerful.

Rather than becoming more androgenous, more alike, our masculinity or femininity becomes enhanced so that we can play the outside game however we want to, without limiting ourselves by being stuck only in one-half our being.

Most of us have not yet learned how to allow our male and female energies to function naturally in the proper relationship with each other. In our culture, we've used our male energy, our ability to think and act, to suppress and control our feminine intuition rather than to support and express her. This traditional use of the male energy I call the "old male." It exists equally in men and women, although it is often more obvious and external in men and more subtle and internal in women. The old male is that part of us that wants to keep control. War is a good example of the old male energy lacking the wisdom and direction of the female. He's terrified of feminine power because he doesn't want to surrender to the power of the universe. He's afraid that if he surrenders he will lose his individual identity.

Another word for the old male is the ego. Its function is to hold on to individuality and separateness at any cost. Therefore, it denies the power of the feminine, which is a force moving toward union and oneness.

In relationship with the old male, the female is helpless in the world. Her power can't move directly into the world. So it often comes out in indirect ways. If we cannot express our female energy through our male energy, then it can come out only indirectly, covertly through manipulation. The energy has to go somewhere; if it doesn't come out directly, it can cause problems for us, even physical illness.

The old male or ego part of us is afraid of the power of the feminine because it's the power of spirit. It's the power of the universe and it feels like it's going to be totally out of control, out of our ego's control. And we're afraid to let go of that control. We're afraid to surrender our ego to the power of the universe and trust that the higher power really does know what to do.

In a sense, the old male is afraid that the power of the female is greater than he is. And in some ways that may be true, but what will counteract this fear is that the more the male within us begins to listen to the female and take action, physical action, the more his strength is increased. He becomes more and more empowered from the power of the female. Eventually we can have physical bodies so flexible and so powerful that we can handle more and more of the universal creative energy coming through us.

The more our male aspect listens to our female aspect and acts on her guidance, the stronger our channel becomes, the more creative energy can flow through it, and the more our bodies can handle it. So we build our strength, we build our clarity, we build our channel every time we listen to our intuitive prompting and take the risk, have the courage to act on it, in every way in our lives, the small things as well as the large.

The small things, in fact, are the most important. For example, when we feel as if we want to say something but we don't say it because we're afraid somebody may not like it, the male in us is failing to carry out the prompting of our inner female. If we can reverse that, even once or twice, it makes a big difference. When you feel you want to say something and you have the courage to go ahead and say it, you feel an empowerment. That feeling is your male aspect listening to your female. When somebody invites you to go somewhere and you don't really want to go, but you do it because you *should*, that is an example of the old male carrying out an action for a reason other than the prompting of the female. But if you feel you don't want to go and your male supports that by saying, "No, I don't want to do that right now," you'll become a little more empowered from that action of trusting yourself.

As men and women, we have played out these old male and female energies in our traditional roles. The traditional role of the male is to be very strong, in control, to cut off his feelings, to be almost like a machine, unemotional, and, in fact, suppressive toward women. That's because internally he's suppressing his own inner female.

The traditional macho man has a helpless, hysterical female voice inside of him desperately trying to be heard. He will tend to attract women who have low self-esteem and are clingy and needy, or who express their power indirectly through manipulation: little girl cuteness, sexual seductiveness, cattiness, or dishonesty.

The traditional role of a woman has been to be emotional and intuitive, but not to be able to empower herself to translate that into action in the world. Therefore, she becomes manipulative; she can't exercise her power directly, so she must exercise it indirectly. She feels helpless and dependent on men.

From this perspective, each person is only half a person, dependent on the other half for its very existence. But because we cannot live healthy lives in the world without the full range of masculine and feminine energies, each sex has been helplessly dependent on the other for its survival. In some ways it may seem like a perfectly workable arrangement. Men help women, women help men. But there is one underlying problem: as an individual, if you don't feel whole, if you feel your survival depends on another person, you are constantly afraid of losing that person. But you know on a deep level that the person you're attracted to is a mirror of yourself. You must not be too dependent on him or her because you know that everything you see in your partner is also in you. You recognize that the reason you're in the relationship is to learn about yourself and deepen your connection with the universe.

I believe that every form of intimate relationship represents each being's attempt to find its feminine and masculine balance within, from the most traditional marriage to open or homosexual or bisexual relationships. I believe that by finding the balance of the male and female within each of us as individuals, we can relate to another person from a place of wholeness: "I am a complete male/female human being and you are mirroring that completion in me. You are mirroring that wholeness in me." And by reflecting each other we can learn from each other.

Many women like myself have had a strongly developed male energy but have used it in the old male way. I was very intellectual, very active, and drove myself very hard to shoulder the responsibilities of the world. I also had a very strongly developed female, but I didn't put her in charge. In fact, I often ignored her. I basically protected my sensitive, vulnerable feelings by erecting a tough outer shell. I've had to learn to take that powerful male energy and use it to listen to, trust, and support my female. This allows her the safety and support to emerge fully. I feel and appear softer, more receptive, and more vulnerable, but now I'm really much stronger.

Women are now learning to validate themselves instead of abandoning their responsibility and getting a man to do it for them. However, they are challenging a deep-seated pattern that has endured for centuries, and it takes time to change it in the deepest layers of our psyche. The key is to keep listening to, trusting, and acting on our deepest feelings.

The union of the male and female within each person allows true love and true passion to come from the universe through each of us. Our relationships can then be based on the love and the passion of the universe rather than on a feeling of inadequacy.

The feminine power, the power of spirit, is always within us. It's up to the ego, our male energy, to determine how we relate to that power. We can either fight it, block it, and attempt to control it

and keep ourselves separate from it, or we can surrender and open to it, trust it, support it, and move
with it.

As each of us deals with this individually, we also
deal with it collectively in our culture and in our
world.

I believe that the world is moving from a position
of fear and distrust of the female power by the male
energy within us to a position of trusting and sup-
porting that power of spirit by the new male within
us, being willing to bring that spirit through and
express it in the world. As each of us makes that
transformation, we see our individual lives beginning to come into balance and harmony. Our relationships begin to reflect that, and eventually the
entire world begins to transform and reflect that.

The power of the feminine energy is on the rise
in our world. As she emerges within us and we
acknowledge and surrender to her, the old male
within us is transformed. He re-emerges, reborn
through the female as the new male, the one who
goes all out in his trust and love for her. He must
grow to become her equal in power so that they can
be the lovers they are meant to be.

I believe the new male has truly been born in our consciousness only within the last few years. Before that we had very little experience in our bodies of the true male energy. Our only concept of the male was the old male. The birth of the new male is synonymous with the birth of the new age. The new world is being built within us and mirrored around us as the new male emerges in all its glory from the feminine power of the spirit.

MEDITATION: CONTACTING YOUR MALE AND FEMALE

Let's take a moment now to contact our male and female aspects.

◇

Find a comfortable position, sitting straight with your back well supported, or lying down comfortably, flat on your back. . . . Close your eyes. Take a deep breath, and as you exhale, relax your body. . . . Take another deep breath, and as you exhale, relax your body more. . . . Take another deep breath, and as you exhale, see if you can relax every part of your body. . . . If there are any areas of your body that still feel tension, put your awareness into those areas. Breathe into them and gently release. . . . Continue to breathe deeply and naturally, and imagine that you can feel the flow of energy all the way through your body, from your toes to the tips of your fingers to the top of your head. . . .

Take another deep breath, and as you exhale, relax your mind. . . . Let each thought that comes into your mind gently float away and allow your mind to slow and come into a soft focus. . . . Take another deep breath, and as you exhale, allow your awareness to move into a very deep, quiet place inside. . . .

Imagine that you are walking down a path in a beautiful place in nature, and as you walk down the path you feel yourself becoming more and more centered, calm, and relaxed. . . . You come to a beautiful place, your inner sanctuary . . . you enter the sanctuary. . . . Take a few moments to feel, see, or experience that beautiful place that is your own private, personal, inner sanctuary. . . . It is very safe and quiet, a place you can visit to feel nurtured and to find quiet time with yourself. . . . Notice what's in your sanctuary: the plants or trees, the water, if there's sun or shade, how warm or how cool it is. . . . Then find a place in your sanctuary to sit down and be very comfortable. . . .

Today you're going to bring into your sanctuary images of your male and female selves. Imagine that you look toward the entrance to the sanctuary, and coming down the path you see or sense a female figure. . . . It could be a woman, a girl, an animal, or it could be a color or a shape or energy. As she approaches the entrance to the sanctuary, see or feel what she looks like, how old or young she is, and how she's dressed. . . . Notice how she moves. . . .

As she comes closer, you begin to feel her energy field. Notice what her energy feels like. . . . She comes near to you now and you greet each other. . . . She has a message she wants to communicate to you. Ask her what she needs to say to you or to communicate to you, whether it be in words or some other form, and then receive whatever you feel her message is. . . . Ask her what she needs or wants from you, either now or in your life in general. . . .

She has a gift to give you. Allow yourself now to receive her gift. . . .

Spend a little time being with her in whatever way feels right for both of you. . . . As you're with her, allow yourself to really feel her energy and imagine that you could bring her energy inside of you and experience it in your body. What does her energy feel like in your body?

Then release her energy from your body and complete your interaction with her for right now in whatever way feels good to you. . . . Ask her if she will stay near you. Perhaps she would like to sit or stand on your left side, whatever feels best for her and for you. . . .

Once again look toward the entrance to your sanctuary and become aware that coming down the path is the figure, the image, or the sense of a male form. . . . This could be a man, a boy, an animal, a color or shape. Begin to see or sense that this is the representation of your inner male energy at this time. As he moves into the sanctuary and comes a little closer, notice more details about what he looks like, how he moves, how he's dressed . . . Begin to feel and sense his energy. . . . As he moves closer, feel his energy more strongly as you see and sense him more clearly. . . .

When he comes close to you, greet each other. He also has a message for you. It may be in words, or it may be communicated in some other way, either telepathically or through actions. Ask him to give you his message . . . and just trust what comes to you. . . . Ask him what he needs from you, either right at this moment or in general in your life. . . .

He, too, has a gift to give you. Allow yourself to receive his gift. . . .

Feel his energy and imagine that you can bring his energy into your body for a moment. Let yourself feel what it feels like to have his energy in your body. . . . Then release his energy from your body and complete your interaction with him for the moment in whatever way feels right. . . .

Now allow your male and female selves to meet each other, to greet each other in whatever way they desire. . . . Ask them if they have something they want to say to each other or communicate to each other in words or in any other way. . . . Ask them if they have anything they need from each other. . . .

Imagine that you can feel both of their energies or each of their energies separately. . . . Imagine that you can bring both energies into your body for a moment. . . . Feel the balance, or the contrast. . . . Then release their energies and allow them to complete their interaction with each other and with you in whatever way feels intuitively right. . . .

When you feel complete with this experience, either ask them to stay with you in the sanctuary for awhile, for however long feels right for all of you, or imagine them moving back up the path and out of the sanctuary, knowing that you can always bring them back whenever you want to, just by wishing for them to come. . . . You can always ask them for advice or help, or ask them to express to you anything that you need to know. . . .

If you want to stay in your sanctuary, stay as long as you desire. If you are ready to leave, begin to move back up the path, and as you walk up the path, feel yourself in a state of balance, centeredness, and vitality. . . . Become aware of your body and of the room around you, and when you feel ready, open your eyes and come back into the room.

DISCOVERING
YOUR
INNER CHILD

◇ ◇ ◇

DISCOVERING
YOUR
INNER CHILD

Most of us think we're supposed to be one consistent personality, and we wonder why we sometimes feel so inconsistent. One day we feel one way, another day we feel another way. Sometimes one minute we feel one way and the next minute we feel a different way. What I've been discovering is that we're not one person at all. We all have many people inside us, many different characters.

Think of these people as being different sub-personalities. Each is distinctly its own character, with its own set of needs and desires, its own point of view, its own opinions. Often these sub-personalities are diametrically opposed to one another. We have a part of us, for example, that thinks the most important thing to do is work very hard and become successful. And if that part of us were running the show we would be working all the time. On the other hand, there may also be a part completely opposite who just wants to relax, hang out, goof off, and enjoy life.

Usually, we're more identified with one or the other of these parts within. If we're a workaholic type of person, we are heavily identified with the character in us that's a hard worker, and we generally ignore, deny, or suppress the other character in us that's perhaps the hedonist, the pleasure lover, or the one that likes to simply *be*. Sometimes we feel the conflict between the two and we bounce back and forth between them.

It's very interesting to get to know all the people inside and to respect them all. Each of them, in fact, is an important part of us. Each is an aspect of our personality that we need to learn to know, respect, explore, and appreciate. By allowing ourselves to know and express *all* the sub-personalities within us, we can become balanced instead of being identified with only one side of a polarity. Ideally, we want to explore both sides of the polarity and then be able to choose the appropriate moments for the different sub-personalities to run the show.

Coming to know all your selves is quite a fascinating exploration. I sometimes think of myself as being a family, not just one person. And as in most families, there's a certain amount of conflict, and there's also a lot of love. The idea is to let every member of the inner family play its role, express itself, and be respected for the part that it plays in the family, so that ultimately the family can be in harmony.

Another interesting metaphor for this situation inside of you is to think of yourself as being a committee. When you think about yourself as a committee, it often explains why it is so difficult for you to get a job done or make a decision. We all know what happens when a decision is made by a committee. One person wants one thing, another wants another, and half the time nothing gets done. If you can get to know the members of your inner committee and allow them to express themselves clearly, then *you*, as a conscious person, can begin to make the decisions, instead of allowing whichever part of you happens to grab control in any given moment make the decisions.

Another way I like to look at this is to think of myself as a theater, and all the characters are playing out their dramas on an inner stage. We tend to attract people into our lives who reflect the various characters inside ourselves—we are attracted to people, and attract people to us, who are similar to our sub-personalities. In this way we play out the inner drama externally. Many lessons in our lives involve learning to see the reflections of people in our lives and what they show us about our inner selves.

The ultimate point is to come to know, love, and accept all aspects of ourselves. There's no part of us that's bad. Everything in the universe wants to be loved and wants to be accepted. Whatever you're not loving and not accepting will follow you around until you love and accept it.

For many of us, for example, it's difficult to accept that there's a person in us that's angry. In fact, it's *really* angry because it's never been listened to and hasn't had a chance to be accepted. But you can start to find safe, comfortable, appropriate ways to allow your anger to be felt and experienced and expressed appropriately, that self eventually becomes an accepted part of you, and a lot of the "charge" dissolves.

Each inner character is very important in our

lives, and each has gifts to give us. But one of the most important aspects of ourselves is our inner child, the child that lives inside each of us always. In fact, we have many children within ourselves. We have within a child of every age, from earliest infancy through adolescence.

These children within have many different aspects. We have a child within that is very vulnerable, very emotional. In fact, the child inside of us is the seat of our emotions. So, to learn to be in contact with our emotions and to love and accept our feelings, we must be in touch with the vulnerable child within us.

There is a child in us that's very playful, that knows how to have fun, just as little children naturally know how to have a good time, know how to play. We all have that child within us, a child that naturally sparkles and has fun and plays and is constantly looking for what's fun in life.

We also have a magical child inside us. This is the part that is naturally tuned in to the magic of the universe. As adults, most of us have forgotten about this magic. When we were children we knew there was magic and we were connected with that magic. We naturally understood the magic of little plants and animals, and maybe we were even in contact with elves and fairies or whatever magic meant to us.

There's also a very wise child within us. It's a part of us that's very truthful, that sees and knows what we're feeling, what other people are feeling, that has the power to cut through much of the superficial dishonesty that exists in adult society, and always goes right to the core truth of situations.

A good way to start to get in touch with or become aware of the child (or many other sub-personalities) within us is to look at real children. Children reflect the child inside us. I'm sure you've all had experiences when you've looked into an infant's eyes and felt a very profound connection. Or you've seen a child be very playful, and it brings out that playful part of you. Or you've had a child say something to you that's so profoundly wise you feel extremely moved by it. You feel that this child in a way knows more than you do. That's a reflection of the knowingness of your inner child.

The child within us is certainly one of the most important aspects of ourselves to contact. One reason is that, as spiritual beings, we come into a physical body and are born into this world as a child, as an infant. So the child is the closest part of our personality to the spiritual essence. When the child is born it is almost purely spiritual essence, because at that point it has no contact or experience with the world. That is why we are so moved when we are with very young children; we see the reflection of our own profound and beautiful and innocent spiritual essence that has not yet been buried or hidden.

As we get in touch with the child inside us, we get in touch with our deepest and purest spiritual essence. By cultivating the relationship with the inner child, we automatically form a deeper and stronger connection with our essence, and our spiritual essence can then come through.

Another important reason for getting in touch with our inner child is that the child is the key to our creativity. We all know how creative children are, unless they've already been inhibited. Very young children are endlessly creative. They're always playing some kind of game of imagination so easily. You know: Let's play house. Let's play fireman. Let's pretend this. Let's pretend that. And they go right into that imaginary world. They're filled with imagination and creativity. They love to draw. They love to paint. They're always singing little songs. They dance. They're magically creative beings.

All of us are that way, too. We all had that magical, creative essence within us as children, but as adults we have suppressed it, we have inhibited it. So, as we get in touch with the child inside us, we release our creativity.

The key to creativity is being willing to try something, to risk doing it and to see what happens. Our creative child is the part of us that's not afraid to try new things. When children draw pictures, they don't worry about whether they're going to look exactly the way some critic thinks they should look. They just do it for the joy of it. And that's how our creative energy can be freed, by feeling the essence of that child within us and being willing to try things that are fun and enjoyable and exciting and new and different. I find over and over again that as people get in touch with the child they open whole new areas of creativity within themselves, which is immensely fun and rewarding.

Also the child is the key to intimacy in relationships. Because the child is the part of us that feels the deepest emotions, it's the part of us that can

truly love. And it's also the part of us that's vulnerable, the part that can be wounded, hurt. To feel
real intimacy with another person you must be in
touch with your vulnerability, with your love, even
with your ability to be wounded.

So, it's the vulnerable child within us that allows
us to feel intimacy and closeness with other people.
If we are not in touch with our child we will not
experience true intimacy. As we learn to be in
touch with the child and take care of the child and
protect and express the child in appropriate ways,
we can experience intimacy in healthy, fulfilling
ways in our lives.

Some people are in touch with their inner child.
Perhaps some of you already know that you are in
touch with your child or you may know people who
are in touch with their child. These people are usually fun to be around or move us emotionally, who
touch us as a child does.

But most of us have suppressed or buried the
child because at a very young age we discovered that
it's not a very safe world for the child. So, from the
very earliest times in our lives we began to build
defenses and protection for the child. Most of our
personality structure, in fact, is a defense, created to

take care of that very sensitive, vulnerable, feeling essence that is the inner child. We build stronger and stronger walls of defense, more and more mechanisms for surviving in a tough world that's not set up for this innocent child.

Eventually, the child that we're trying to protect gets totally buried inside us, and we don't even know it exists. That's the predicament most of us are in. We automatically run on our defense systems and our survival mechanisms, and we forget that the reason we have them is to take care of and fulfill the needs of the child. But the child inside us is in pain because its needs are not being met. The child does not go away. It never grows up. It never dies. It is with us through our entire lives.

If we're not conscious of those needs, then we are constantly trying to fulfill them unconsciously. The child within is unconsciously motivating all our behavior. We may, for example, develop a sub-personality that's a workaholic because it's trying to make enough money to make the child feel safe and protected. But we end up forgetting about the child and spend our whole lives working hard. We may accumulate a lot of money and a lot of success, but none of it gives us the satisfaction we need because we've forgotten about the child who was the original motivating force.

Sometimes the child will actually sabotage our attempts to be successful or do the things we think we should do, because secretly the child knows that its needs are not going to be met by what we're striving for. I've found that when people have a block about being successful in life, often the block comes from the inner child whose needs are not being met. The child will stop you from being successful until you start to give it more nurturing, more love, more time to play, or whatever it needs.

So our challenge is to get in touch with the inner child, to find out what the child's needs are, and to begin consciously to take care of the child. The child's needs are for love, for physical and emotional contact, for enjoyment, and to express itself honestly and creatively. As we begin to find ways of doing those things, we find our whole personality starts to come into alignment, and we become healthy and balanced.

There are many ways to get in touch with the child inside us: through playing, dancing, singing, drawing, painting, by being in nature, or by hanging out with children and allowing ourselves to ex-

perience our inner child. Buy a toy, a stuffed animal, and allow your inner child to express what it
wants and needs in ways that are fun. Often the
child inside comes forth with animals, because
children naturally love animals.

One way that's been very helpful for many people
is through the meditation that follows.

MEDITATION:
CONTACTING YOUR
INNER CHILD

Before starting this meditation, be sure you create the most positive possible environment for the safety and comfort of the child. Find a place that feels very comfortable and private. You may want to have a blanket, a stuffed animal, or something else that will make your child feel welcome. You may want to meditate outdoors in a special place or find a special place in your house that feels nurturing to you.

When you first do this meditation it's important to keep a few things in mind. Sometimes, even though we have spent most of our lives not being in touch with our inner child, our first attempt will be very easy. The child has been waiting for us and wanting that contact with us. But sometimes the child is not yet ready to trust us, so it may take a little patience. The child may hold back until it knows that you really want this contact and that you're willing to be responsible and consistent with the contact.

When you first do this meditation, trust what comes, trust what happens. If the child is a little reserved or a little hesitant, just give the child time. Keep doing the meditation regularly and you'll find that the contact will continue to increase and become stronger and more positive. For now, though, simply accept whatever happens.

It may be that you'll get in touch with a child who's very emotional, sad, or hurt. Or, you may get in touch with a child who's very playful and wants to be with you and have fun. You may be in touch with the magical aspect of your child, or with the wise child. Accept what comes to you, because that will be the part that's ready to be discovered at this time. As you continue to work with this meditation you may discover different aspects of the child. Trust your own experience.

◇

Get comfortable, either sitting or lying down. If you're sitting up, be sure your back is supported so you can sit straight. If you're lying down, lie down comfortably, flat on your back. Close your eyes. . . . Take a deep breath, and as you exhale, relax your body. . . . Take another deep breath, and as you exhale, relax your body deeper and deeper. . . . Take another deep breath, and as you exhale, imagine relaxing your body as completely as you can. Your whole body is now completely relaxed. . . .

Take another deep breath, and as you exhale, relax your mind. . . . Let your thoughts float away; let your mind come into stillness and quiet. . . . Take another deep breath, and as you exhale, imagine moving your awareness into a deep, quiet place inside of you. . . .

Then imagine that you're walking down that beautiful path to your inner sanctuary. . . . And as you walk down the path you feel more and more relaxed, centered, and comfortable. You enter your sanctuary and sense and feel the beauty and comfort of nature all around you. . . .

Take a few moments to get in touch with your sanctuary, to remember some of the details about this place and to let yourself enjoy being there. . . . Imagine that you're walking around your sanctuary noticing the various plants and animals, feeling the sun or the breeze, and a little way off in the distance, across the sanctuary, you become aware of the presence of a small child. . . . As you start to move toward the child, you see or sense whether it's a boy or girl, about how old it is, and what the child is doing. . . .

Slowly move toward the child, and as you get closer notice how the child is dressed. . . . Allow yourself to sense how the child is feeling emotionally. . . . Approach the child and make contact in whatever way you sense would be appropriate right now. . . .

Ask the child if there is anything it wants to tell you or wants to communicate to you. It may be in words or it may be in some other way. Allow yourself to receive whatever the child wants to communicate. . . .

Now ask the child what it needs most from you, right now or in your life in general. . . . Listen to what the child has to tell you, whether in words or in other ways. . . .

Spend a little time being with your child. . . . Allow the child to guide you in the appropriate way to be with it, whether playing together or simply sitting close or holding each other. . . .

The child has a special gift to give you. Allow yourself now to receive the gift the child has for you. . . .

Continue to be with your child. . . . Let the child know that you want to be in contact with it as much as you can from now on. . . .

Complete your time together for right now in whatever way feels good for both of you. You and the child have a choice to make. The child can choose to remain here in the sanctuary, in a very safe place inside of you, and you can come to visit the child in your sanctuary. Or, the child can come with you when you leave the sanctuary. Your child will know which way feels best for right now, and it can always change in the future.

If the child is going to stay in the sanctuary, say goodbye for now. Let the child know that you will come back as often as you can, and that you want to know how the child feels and what it needs from you in your life. . . .

If the child is coming with you, take it in your arms or by the hand and start to walk up the path out of the sanctuary. As you walk up the path, feel yourself alive, filled with energy, balanced, and centered. . . .

Become aware of your body in the room, and when you feel ready, open your eyes and come back into the room.

◇

Now that you've gotten in touch with your inner child, it's important to follow through and be consistent in taking care of and being present with this child on a regular basis. You are the parent to your own inner child. It's important to become a conscious, loving, responsible parent to that child. This can be enjoyable for you and for the child, but it also requires some awareness and responsibility on your part. It means that you need to start making some space in your life for that child at appropriate times.

If you're not sure what the needs of your child are or how to best take care of your child, simply ask. The child knows what it wants and what it needs at all times, so cultivate the habit of communicating with the child, asking what it needs, what it wants. Then do your best to give that child the fulfillment of its needs. You can't always do everything the child wants when it wants, but you should include its needs in your life, just as you would with a real child. Make them as much a priority as you can, and you will find that the rewards are great.

Start to think about things that are fun or that are nurturing for the child, and begin to include them in your life in a regular way. Every day, or at least every couple of days, take some time, even if it's just a few minutes in the morning or a few minutes in the evening, and find out what your child likes to do. Get toys the child likes to play with, go for walks, ride a bike, take hot bubble baths, get story books—things that really feed and nurture your inner child. Of course, the most important thing to the child is love and intimacy, so your child will guide you in finding more contact, closeness, friendship, and love with other people.

It's also important to learn when it's not appropriate to bring your child out. In the middle of a business meeting at work is probably not the best time to have your child come out. You can allow your child to stay home and play. Just tell the child that you're going off to work and that you'll be home later on, and that you'll take some time to play then.

Even though these things may feel a little silly at first, they will end up bringing much more balance, harmony, enjoyment, and fulfillment into your life.

EXPRESSING
YOUR
CREATIVITY

◇ ◇ ◇

EXPRESSING
YOUR
CREATIVITY

Many people think they're not creative. I hear this all the time in my workshops; people say to me, "I'm not creative." I don't believe it. I've found from working with many people that, after we get through our limited ideas and our blocks and our fears, we are all creative beings. I don't know what more proof we need of our creativity than to look at our lives and realize that, on a metaphysical level, we have created them. Granted, they're not perfect, but they are nevertheless a powerful manifestation of our creativity. We need to acknowledge how incredible our lives really are and therefore how incredible we are. We have all created an enormous amount of powerful, interesting, even amazing experiences and people in our lives. And those are all mirrors of our creativity.

We create our own reality every moment, whether or not we're conscious of it. If we're not conscious, we create it out of habit and old patterns. As we become more and more conscious, we are more able to create what we truly desire.

I find that the idea that we are not creative usually comes from some type of early programming or conditioning that we've received. Somebody along the way told us we weren't creative, and we believed it. Or maybe we got so much criticism or disapproval or not enough encouragement and support to express our natural creativity, that we came to the conclusion that we weren't creative.

Many people tend to equate creativity with only certain types of expression. We all know that art or dance or music is creative, for example, but we don't necessarily think that running a business is creative, or running a home is creative, or that being a parent is creative. And yet, when you think about it, what could be more creative than raising children? That is the ultimate creative act. To create another human being and to learn how to support that human being in expressing his or her creativity is probably the ultimate challenge. Cooking is creative. Many of our recreational activities, and even the little things that we do all the time, are very creative. But because they come easily to us and they're natural, we don't usually think of them as being creative.

Start to think about the things you do that are enjoyable, that come naturally and easily to you, and see the creative aspect of those expressions, see how those are a truly important expression of your being. Try taking some risks. Do some new and different things that you find creative. I've noticed that a lot of people have the concept that they're too old to try something new, especially something "creative"—if they didn't start it when they were children or very young people, they figure it's too late to do it now.

I always encourage people to fantasize, to think about creative things they would like to do. See if there is something you can do, a step you can take in the direction of those fantasies, even if they seem a bit far-fetched. It's never too late.

We know that each of us is in essence a creative being, a spiritual being who comes into a physical form. That physical form is our first act of creation.

We create a body to express our spirit. I know that a lot of us don't like our bodies and don't think they're the best creation we could have made, but our bodies, in fact, are in a constant state of creative change. As we are changing internally, our bodies, as the expression of our spirit, are also changing. So the more you come to know, acknowledge, and express your creative spirit, the more your spirit shows in your primary creative project—your body.

Start to look at your body as your creation and see how it expresses your spirit. Observe the ways that you block yourself from expressing your spirit and see how that is reflected in your body. As you remove these blocks to your creative expression, your body will reflect that transformation.

As adults, the major block to our creativity is our inner critic, that part of us that internally criticizes what we do. We have standards of perfection incorporated from the world around us, ways that we think things *should* be done. We have a critic within who criticizes us when we are not doing things the way we feel that should be done. For most of us, this inner critic is what stops us from taking the kinds of risks that need to be taken to be creative.

Creativity requires experimentation. The fundamental principle of creativity is that you do something, you express something, you *try* something. And you must be willing to allow things to be expressed that are not particularly wonderful or perfect or just the way you think they should be expressed. You have to let the expressions flow. People who are creative are willing to make mistakes. Almost all successful persons say that they have had more failures than they've had successes. They have tried many things that have not always worked for them. Some have been very disappointing, but they have continued to take risks and try again.

What stops us from being successful is the critic inside that says, "You're not very smart," "You're not very talented," "You don't know how to do this right," "You're not as good as so-and-so," "You're not as good as you should be," or "Look at what you did, that's not any good," "That's ridiculous," "That's inadequate." We all have, to some degree, that self-criticism. Those of us who have allowed our creativity to flow in our lives have managed in one way or another to set our critic aside long enough to let the energy come through spontaneously.

Dealing with the inner critic is difficult; there's

no simple solution. The first step is to recognize your internal critic, to begin to notice what it says to you, and to begin to get in touch with where the voice came from. For most of us, it began very early in our lives when we were children, when we received criticism from our parents or our siblings or our teachers or those around us, who said, "You don't do that well enough," or "You didn't do that right," or "You're a bad boy or girl," and we've incorporated that criticism. Beginning to become aware of your inner critic, to acknowledge it and notice where it came from, can start to free you from automatically believing it.

It doesn't seem to help very much simply to try to make the critic shut up. The critic is a strong voice inside us. The key is to begin to notice it and to think to yourself, "Now, do I need to believe this?" "Is this really true?" "Do I have to let this run my life?" "Do I have to let this stop me?"

By asking these questions you can eventually get to a place where you listen to the critic, you acknowledge what it has to say, and then you go ahead and do what you want to do anyway. You could say to yourself: "Okay, critic, thank you for sharing your point of view. Now I'm going to go ahead and do this, and even if it isn't perfect, I'm going to do it anyway because I think it'll be fun, or because I want to try something new and I'm willing to let myself be like a child. I'm willing to play, try something and risk and experiment and learn in the process. If I don't do it perfectly, fine; I'll do it again and I'll do it better next time. Or I'll forget it and do something else. It doesn't really matter."

Creativity requires play. It requires fun. It requires a sense of adventure. Learn to look at things a little more lightly and not take them so seriously. If we take ourselves too seriously we can't have that adventurousness that allows us to explore in new places.

One good way to deal with the critic and begin to free more of your creativity is by using some clearing processes. If you have a journal or if you want to start a journal, try writing your creative voice and then writing any blocks or inhibitions you have about that creative voice. Or try writing the voice of your critic. Write it all down so you can see objectively what it is that stops you, what concepts of yourself you have that stop you from being able to be creative.

Here's a suggestion for starting the flow of your

creativity, getting in touch with how you block yourself, and being able to start to clear some of those blocks. Think of something you've always wanted to do that you think of as creative, something you've never tried or that you've never thought you could do. For example, if you don't consider yourself an artist think about drawing a picture.

Get your materials together: paper, pencils, or whatever you're going to use for your drawing. Tune into whatever feelings you have inside that are stopping you, that are telling you you can't draw or that you won't be able to do it well enough. Then take a piece of paper and a pen or pencil and write down all the self-critical or doubting voices or feelings you have inside. For example: "I'm going to waste this paper because I'm such a terrible artist," or "I just don't know how to do this," or "It's going to look really stupid." Write down whatever you are feeling.

Then allow your more creative voice to express itself, and write down what it tells you. It may be something like, "Well, it doesn't really matter how well I do this, I just want to do it because it'll be fun," or "I just want to try taking these colors and putting them on this paper to see what it looks like," or "I just want to experiment with this." Keep that dialogue going for a little while until you feel you've cleared enough of a space to try drawing. Then go ahead and draw.

Carry on the same sort of dialogue until you clear the space enough so you can feel that you're enjoying what you're doing. It doesn't matter what the result is. The purpose of your creative energy is for your own enjoyment. It's to feel the feeling of being a channel and to allow that creative force to come through you. That is very pleasurable in itself. If you keep that focus in everything you do, you will begin to de-emphasize the necessity for doing things perfectly or producing an exact result—and you will begin to get the same kind of pleasure out of life that children do when they are spontaneously moving with their energy and doing what they feel.

Many people are creative in one area of their lives, but not in other areas. If you have one area in which you're creative, you have an advantage in that you know what it's like to allow that creative channel to flow. Think about whatever it is you do in that aspect of your life. If you play music or you're creative in business, what is it that allows you to be creative? How do you get your critic out of the way? How do you trust yourself and express yourself? Think about how you can take the same method you use in your creative area and apply it in other areas of your life, how you can apply it with something new or different so that you allow your creativity to flow in a new direction.

One of the most important aspects of getting in touch with creativity are your fantasies, dreams, and visions. Some people come to workshops and say to me, "Oh, I don't have any fantasies or visions." But I find, after questioning, that *everybody* has fantasies and dreams and visions. The reason some people think they don't is because they invalidate them. They think, "Oh, well, that's nothing," or "That's so foolish it isn't even worth thinking about." Or the fantasies are unconscious and people don't realize they're having them.

Everybody has fantasies about what they want to do, about what they love to do, about what they would do if only they could. So, give yourself a chance to fantasize freely. Enjoy it! If you could have all the money in the world, what would you like to do? If you could do anything you wanted to do, what would it be? Also ask yourself: What kinds of things do I love doing? What comes easily to me? What's fun? What do I do so naturally that I don't even think about it? How could I expand it? How could I possibly make a living from doing the things that I think are the most enjoyable and the most fun? Try not to limit yourself. Be open to all kinds of possibilities that you've never allowed yourself to imagine before.

Some of our fantasies, of course, turn out to be impractical. But I've found that for the most part, the recurring fantasies and dreams we have in our lives contain a great deal of truth. They show us something important about our creative selves: what our purposes are in our lives, what we came here to do, what we want to express. Give yourself a chance to explore and express those fantasies, in your own mind, through writing, through drawing, through talking to a friend, through visualizing. And then ask yourself, "What are some very small, simple steps I can take toward realizing those fantasies?" Even though you may not see how you can pursue your fantasies, ask yourself if there's some simple step you can take in their direction. And then, go ahead; take a risk and do it. See what happens. If it doesn't work out, that's fine. Try something else.

Chances are you will discover a whole new creative aspect of your life.

As you start to express your creativity in new ways, don't aim too high and get discouraged. Start with small things. Let yourself take a step that's fun and relatively easy and enjoyable, and then appreciate yourself for that. If you keep taking small steps you will end up being exactly where you need to be. For example, after you finish reading this section, try thinking of one thing that you can do in your life, today or tomorrow, that would express your creativity in a way that you wouldn't normally consider. You could rearrange your room, for example, in a way that makes your environment a little more creative. Or you could look in your closet and put on the clothes that feel like they would express you in a new and different way today. Or make some other small change in your life.

Then continue looking for little ways to express yourself more creatively and differently. Have fun with it. If you've always wanted to play a musical instrument, or dance, or learn to sail, enroll in a class. Even if you don't think you have the talent or the ability, try it and see what happens.

What it really boils down to is this: You can do things in the same old way you've always done them, which is safe and secure, but also a little bit dull and boring, or you can try something new and different. You may learn something, and you may have some fun. So why not go for the fun?

MEDITATION: CONTACTING YOUR CREATIVITY

Here is a meditation to help you get in touch with your creativity. In this meditation, let your imagination open, and trust whatever comes to you. Enjoy it.

◇

Find a comfortable place to sit or lie down. Close your eyes.

Relax. . . . Take a deep breath, and as you exhale, relax your body. . . . Take another deep breath, and as you exhale, relax your body more deeply. . . . Take another deep breath, and as you exhale, relax your body completely. . . . Feel the energy flowing freely through your body as you breathe. . . .

As you inhale, imagine that you're breathing in the life force of the universe. Imagine it coming into every cell of your body. . . . As you exhale, release all the old limitations, fears, and doubt that you no longer need. Every time you exhale, you release the old and make room for the new. . . . And as you inhale you bring in fresh, creative energy. . . .

Take another deep breath, and as you exhale, relax your mind. . . . Imagine that all your old, limited ideas about yourself are floating away. Imagine that all your old conditioning and programming about who you are and who you aren't, about what you can do and what you can't do, are all dissolving and floating away. You are an unlimited being, and you are now open to new ideas, new feelings, and new inspirations. . . .

Take another deep breath, and as you exhale, allow your awareness to move into a deep place inside of you. . . . With each breath imagine going deeper and deeper, until you come to rest in a quiet place inside. . . .

Now imagine that you are walking down a beautiful path toward your inner sanctuary. . . . As you walk

down the path toward your sanctuary, you are feeling very open and alive, almost like a new person,
ready to have new experiences and new adventures,
and to discover something new about yourself. . . .

Enter your sanctuary and take a few moments to
experience being there. . . . Notice what's in your
sanctuary, how it looks, how it feels. You may find
there's something different about it today, or it may
be the same as usual. . . . Allow yourself to feel the
peace and nurturing and safety of being in your
sanctuary. . . . Find a place to sit down and be
comfortable. . . .

Today we're going to invite your creative being, the
most creative part of yourself, to come into your
sanctuary with you. Look toward the entrance of
your sanctuary and begin to sense or visualize your
creative being coming down the path. . . . This is
some part of you that is very creative. It may be a
part that you've been in touch with before, or it may
be some part of you that you've never seen or experienced before. Just trust whatever comes to you
in your imagination now. . . .

As this creative being comes into your sanctuary, begin to see or sense who it is, what it looks like. . . . It could be a person, a man or woman, an animal, a color or shape, or anything that comes to your mind. . . . Notice the details about your creative being. Let yourself be open to its appearing in whatever way it wishes. . . .

Now your creative being comes toward you and you make contact with each other. . . . Allow yourself to feel the energy of this creative being. . . . Ask the being what message it has for you or what it wants to tell you or communicate to you, whether in words or in any other way. . . . Ask your creative being what it most wants to do, how it wants to express itself in your life. . . . Also ask your creative being how it already expresses itself in your life. . . . Ask if there's anything it would like to do with you right now, and go ahead and be together in whatever way feels good or right. . . .

Your creative being wants to take you somewhere. Allow yourself to be guided by your creative being on a little journey through your sanctuary, to an area that you've never seen before. . . . In this new place there is a beautiful pool of clear, warm water. Your creative being lets you know that this is a pool of your own creative energy. Take your clothes off and slowly enter the pool and let yourself float in the warm water. . . .

As you float in the pool, look up and watch the sky gradually become a night sky, with bright stars shining. . . . You see one star that's particularly bright, and you know that this is your special star. . . . The star has something to tell you about the purpose of your life at this time. Listen to what the star has to say to you. . . .

When you feel ready to emerge from the pool, step out of the water. . . . You will find that your clothes have disappeared and your creative being has brought you new clothes that are very special and magical. Your creative being dresses you in these new clothes. . . . The clothes feel wonderful, as though they are expressing an essence of who you are. Let yourself move freely, and just notice how your body feels in these clothes. . . . If it feels right to you, you might even dance with your creative being in a dance that feels like a true expression of how you feel. . . .

When you feel complete, you and your creative being move back to your familiar place in the sanctuary. . . . Ask if there are any steps your creative being wants you to take in your life right now. . . . Then ask if there's anything further your creative being wants to express to you at this time. . . .

If you want to stay in your sanctuary and stay with your creative being, you may continue to do so as long as you desire. . . . If you're ready to leave, you and your creative being can walk together out of the sanctuary and up the path. . . . As you walk up the path, feel your creative being with you, as a part of you that you can invoke in your life anytime you wish. . . .

Become aware of your body and of your presence in the room. . . . When you feel ready, open your eyes and come back into the room.

◇

If you wish, take some paint, colored pens, or crayons and make a picture of your creative being and/

or of your inner sanctuary. Don't worry about how perfect the picture is or isn't. Let your creative inner child draw the picture. Hang it on your wall or put it in your notebook to help you remember and express that creativity within you.